Howdy

and welco...

Thanks

for coughing up the $13.

I REALLY love Moab.
It is a bizarre, quirky place with lotsa great people, places, and of course, THE BEST riding on the planet. If you get immediate pleasure knowing there is grass (or weeds) 6 inches off both sides of your tires, you may not like this place. But if you like rocks, technical challenges and traction that is simply indescribable, you'll never shake this place from your blood. I know I can't.

I've done my best to put together a guide that gives you a range of rides from easy to extreme, with descriptions to help you choose. Heck, I say "do 'em all!" My maps are a little scary, but so is mountain biking. The actual routes are pretty bang-on, but objects/cliffs are drawn to give you points of reference. I think they're pretty useful, but they are no substitute for experience, skill and common sense.

The Yellow Pages section is there for your reference, either when in town or planning your next trip.

Have Fun!
Cheers!

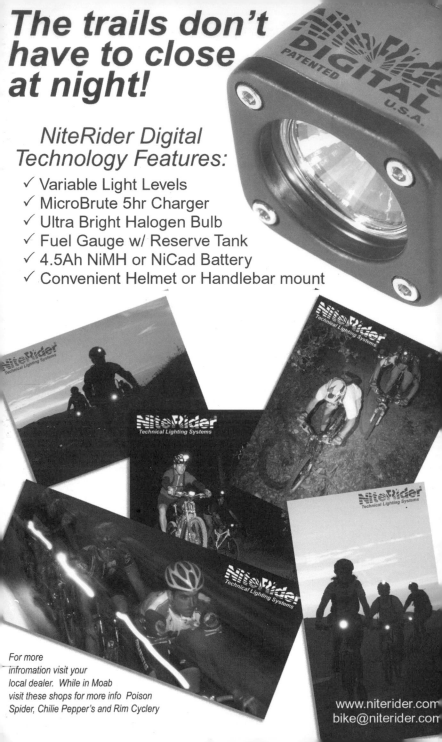

Table of Contents

E - Easy   M - Moderate   T - Tough

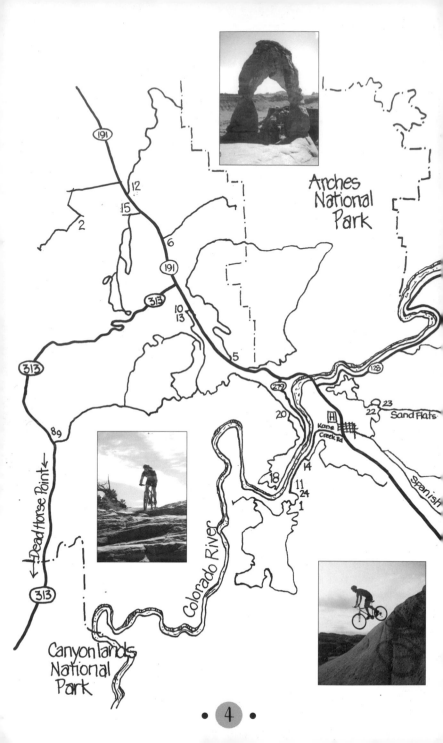

Arches
National
Park

191

12

15

2

6

191

313

10
13

5

313

128

279

20

Kane
Creek Rd

23

22

Sand Flats

89

18

14

11
24

1

← Dead Horse Point ←

313

Spanish

Colorado River

Canyonlands
National
Park

Trail List

1. Amasa Back
2. Bartlett Wash
3. Burro Pass
4. Canyonlands Overlook
5. Courthouse Loop
6. Dalton Wells
7. Flat Pass
8. Gemini Bridges
9. Gemini ~ Eagles Perch
10. Gold Bar Rim
11. Hurrah Pass
12. Klondike Bluffs
13. Little Canyon Rim
14. Moab Rim
15. Monitor & Merrimac
16. Moonlight Meadow
17. North Beaver Mesa
18. Poison Spider Mesa
19. Porcupine Rim
20. Pu'lal Trail
21. Schuman's Gulch
22. Slickrock Trail
23. Slickrock Practice
24. Spring Race Course
25. Top of the World

Ⓗ Hospital

Rider Mel's Mountain Bike Guide to Moab
Trail List

Entrada Bluffs Rd.

Colorado River

128

128

Fisher Valley Rd.

Castle Valley Road

17

19

Ken's Lake

7

La Sal Mtn. Loop

21

Oowah Lk. Rd.

3

Geyser Pass Rd.

16

191

4

©Rider Mel 2000

N

SCALE
1 mile

Riding in the Desert

Okay Homeboy, riding in the desert just isn't like riding elsewhere. Here are a few keys to getting maximum fun and getting out alive.

1. Bring as much water as you can carry. You need at least two large water bottles or a large Camelbak bladder in spring and fall.

In summer, temps often exceed 100°F (38°C) with very little shade. Start riding at sunrise and bring at least 100 ounces of water – more if at all possible! I recommend two full Camelbak bladders! It is absolutely insane to try riding mid-day in the summer – I'm talking nasty, heat stroke, blood-congealing death.

Bring some form of food in all seasons. I recommend sports bars (you know the brands), granola bars, dried fruit, and beef jerky – especially if you've killed and dried the animal yourself. If you can, bring a steak sandwich (use tenderloin and provolone cheese) with onions, lettuce, tomatoes, hot peppers, and "secret sauce" (we all know its really just Italian dressing). You may want to wash all this down with a nice wine – try the Cakebread Cellars Chardonnay.

2. Watch the weather. Desert weather is tough to predict and often vicious. Storms often mean flash floods and lightning – either one can equal death very quickly. I have tried crouching on the ground getting hammered with rain, thunder and lightening – believe me, you don't want to try it. Use the forecasts and keep your eyes and ears open to signs of a storm. Carry a rainjacket in spring/summer/fall and a fleece in colder months.

Always know where you are and how to get out quickest. You must be willing to "bail" on a ride - live to ride another day. In the spring and fall (and especially the winter) storms can bring hail, snow, and occasionally Santa Claus. Be prepared (bring warm clothing, fire-starting materials, plum pudding).

3. Pay attention to the maps, trail markers and your overall orientation (that's North, South, etc, Bub). Know the route and directions before you start. Remember, maps are great but no substitute for common sense. Sometimes bozos steal trail markers (don't be a bozo).

If you lose the trail:
❶ Backtrack. You were once on it and should be able to find it again (and the correct way out). ❷ Spiral outwards looking for signs of other riders, trail, or Jeeps. ❸ NEVER try to descend off trail into a canyon or do anything to reduce your visibility to potential rescuers – they are very good at what they do if they know roughly where you are and you don't hide all clues.

4. Know your limitations and those of others in your group. Probably better to hurt some feelings than visit the hospital or worse. Moab trails are NOT for beginners. Besides, Moab offers piles of fun for non-riders: hiking in any number of spots (including the biking trails), watching kids skate, BMX, or in-line at the park, shopping for trinkets, sipping espresso, hanging out.

5. Carry tools and know how to use them. Riding on rock is amazing. It also does amazing things to your bike. Simply put, shit breaks (often). At the very least, I recommend:

- multi-tool(or allen key set and chain tool)
- spoke wrench (but only use as required)
- pump
- tire levers
- lube
- spare tubes (and patch kit)
- compass
- duct tape
- toilet paper
  (like I said, shit happens)
- sunscreen
- flashlight
- lighter
- reflective "tent tape"
- money and identification

—After ANY ride—

where you've had a mechanical problem, go see a bike shop ASAP. MacGuyver-style trail repairs are great and often turn a mess into a fun ride, but let a professional finish the job right.

DISCLAIMER

Mountain biking is NOT a safe sport – ask anyone. Scrapes and bruises happen frequently – so do stitches and broken bones. Use good judgement, maps, a compass, experienced friends/guides. Ask about the trails and trail conditions in a local bike shop and with the BLM. Everyone gets lost every now and then – stay calm, use your brain. I've tried hard to describe and map trails accurately. BUT, I cannot be responsible for: trail changes, missing markers, bad weather, missing brain cells, wild animals, testosterone-charged stupidity, or your buddy's beer farts. If you want to ride, take responsibility to know: what you're doing, where you're going, and the forecasted weather. Let someone know where you're riding and when you expect to be back. NEVER skimp on water. Know how to deal with basic mechanical problems. Be prepared to walk out – it happens to everyone sooner or later.
And remember, you're having fun, SMILE!

Ride Ratings

I have done my best to describe each trail in terms of its physical difficulty, technical difficulty and potential to scare the heck out of you. These are subjective ratings made by me, a pretty fit, mid 30's male with a masochistic tendency and a wife and kids to go home to. The scale used is 1 to 10 (with 11 indicating something truly extreme). I have also tried to briefly outline why the rating was given.

Grunt Factor
Physical difficulty comes from mileage, amount and difficulty of climbs, and severity of trail surface.

Techno Factor
Technical difficulty comes from the number and degree of obstacles, and bike-handling skills required.

Fear Factor
"Fear Factor" comes from the amount (and degree) of scary stuff. Basically, this comes down to exposure to cliff edges, nasty rock drops, and severity of slope or grade.

Looking for something specific?

These "stamps" will give you
at-a-glance info to help you choose.

Classic Rides

Rider Mel's favorite
Moab rides! These
make me feel all warm
and fuzzy.

Giggle Rides

Off-road fun for the
whole family. Not too
tough, but piles of
fun. Second ride of
the day?

Moses Rides

Wander-around-the-
desert-for- 40-years
kind of riding. Likely
to prompt visions of
god or epiphanies
(like "what the hell
was I thinking?")

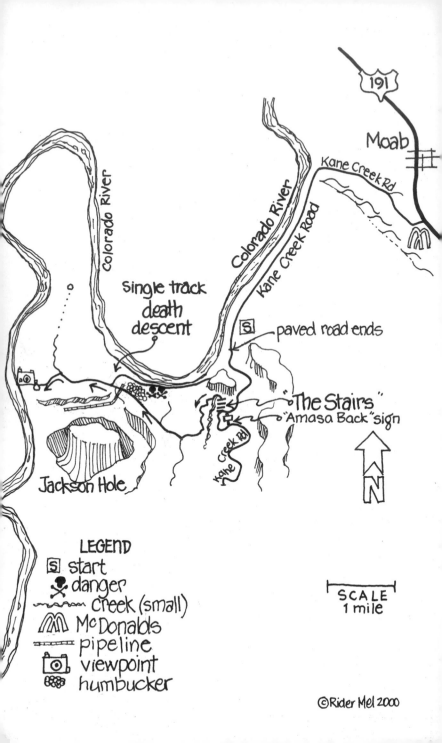

Amasa Back

killer views
killer rides

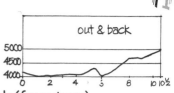

out & back

Distance:	21 Miles out and back (from town)
Time Required:	3 Hours
Grunt Factor:	(8) Pretty tough climb "out", rockin fun "back"
Techno Factor:	(8) Difficult in spots, lots ' o' lifts/drops
Fear Factor:	(7) "The Stairs" + others, but your chamois should stay dry
Route Finding:	Pretty easy, look for the cairns (neat little piles of rock)
Season:	Any, provided you like 100°F without shade. Best spring and fall. Bring water! Early morning in the summer.

Description: Definitely one of The Classic Moab rides. This Out and Back has everything a Bitter, GenX, Thrash-a-holic Bikehead could want: a rock staircase, stream crossing, climbs/descents with technical moves, awesome overlook viewpoint, and a martini bar at the top. Okay, just kidding about the stream crossing! The trail basically drops in RIGHT off the gravel road at a spot I call "The Stairs". You cross a small creek and the climb begins. You pretty much follow the ledge up to the top of Amasa Back. Check out Jackson's Hole on your left as you level out near the top. It's basically a canyon with a large butte in the middle. Be careful on the 2-track - it approaches a series of BIG drops, called Humbucker, which is absolutely heinous and could kill you. Locals may describe a few different lines through this mess. I simply pick up my bike and CAREFULLY walk through it! Soon after Humbucker you'll ride over a pipeline followed by two spurs. The first spur (left) takes you to Jacob's Ladder, a ridiculous hike-a-bike down to Jackson Hole. The second spur (right) takes you to a ballistic singletrack descent listed below. Near the top look for rock cairns and the overlook ledge. If you go too far it's kinda tough to turn back! On the return keep your eyes peeled for the trail – it's easy to lose if you're really movin'.

Amasa Back
— continued —

Options: Those who love steep, loose, nasty singletrack descents with "big death on the left" can take the first RIGHT after you ride over the big pipeline (near the top). Definitely technical, scary and perfect for those who aren't quite right. If you're planning to ride this route check with a local shop - the Creek crossing can be more dangerous than the trail in high water.

Directions: From Main x Center head SOUTH on HWY 191. Turn RIGHT at McDonalds onto Kane Creek Rd. Stay on Kane Creek past the Scenic Chairlift and around the curve. Go past the Moab Rim trailhead parking lot on your left. If you drove, park in the lot just before the cattle gate (where the pavement ends). Ride up the gravel road for about 1 mile to the trailhead on the RIGHT.

LEGEND
start
view
Avoid when wet!
191
Blue Hills Rd.
gravel
Moab
views (everywhere)
wash
slick rock
2m.
"Big" Steep Ramp Up!
sand dunes
N
SCALE
1 mile
©Rider Mel 2000

Bartlett Wash

slickrock
playground

Distance: 5 Miles out-and-back + slickrock freeform riding

Time Required: 1 - 2 Hours plus whatever your heart desires

Grunt Factor: Tough as you make it (4 Minimum)

Techno Factor: Tough as you make it (5 Minimum)

Fear Factor: Scary as you make it (5 Minimum)

Route Finding: Short trail out to playground.

Season: Spring/Fall. Very hot in the summer (unless you ride very early). Never drive out to this trail under threat of rain – you could be there for quite a while.

Description: Bartlett Wash is a short ride from the campground to a slickrock playground that is as easy or tough as you make it. It makes an incredibly good slickrock practice area, or spot for super-cool photos. Pay attention – don't act like a 14 year-old watching their first porno. Danger can really "sneak up on you". Also, traction can be inconsistent across the color spectrum of slickrock. Remember, the best crashes normally occur when the camera comes out!

Directions: From town, drive North on Hwy 191 for about 17 miles. Just before mile marker 143 turn LEFT on the dirt road (Blue Hills Rd.). After just over 2 miles take the spur to the LEFT as the road bends to the right. In less than a mile, turn LEFT at the  3-way intersection. Just past that is another road to the right. Go straight past. Go through the wash and take your first RIGHT. Park in the lot and ride your bike through the gate, picking up the singletrack (and steep rock climb up) to the slickrock.

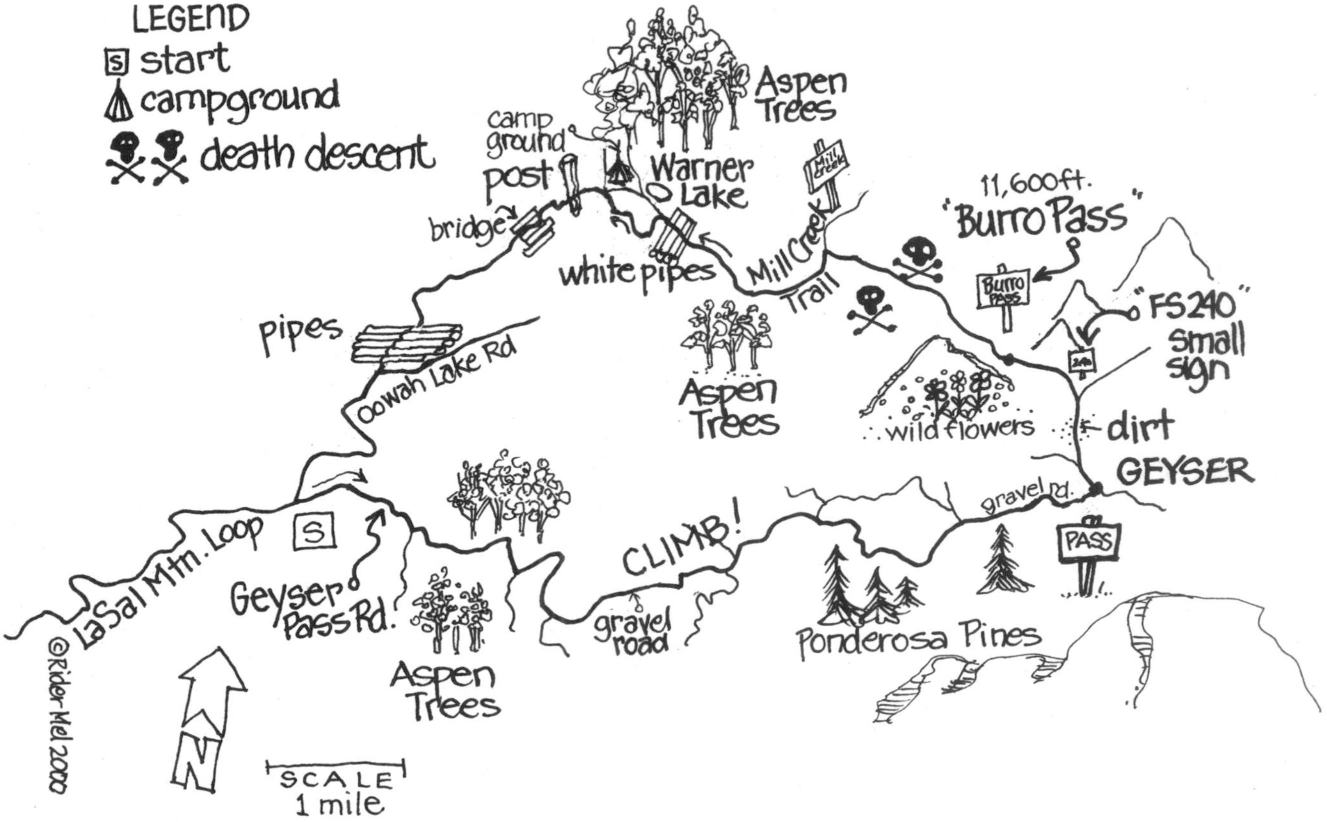
LEGEND
S start
campground
death descent
camp ground
post
bridge
Aspen Trees
Warner Lake
white pipes
Mill Creek
Mill Creek Trail
11,600 ft.
"Burro Pass"
Burro Pass
"FS 240"
small sign
pipes
Oowah Lake Rd
Aspen Trees
wild flowers
dirt
GEYSER
gravel rd.
PASS
S
LaSal Mtn. Loop
Geyser Pass Rd.
CLIMB!
gravel road
Ponderosa Pines
Aspen Trees
N
SCALE
1 mile
©Rider Mel 2000

Burro Pass

monster-tough adventure in the La Sals

Chart showing elevation profile: y-axis 7,500 to 11,500 ft, x-axis 0 to 19, labeled "loop"

Distance:	19 Mile loop
Time Required:	4 - 6 Hours
Grunt Factor:	(11) VICIOUS 10-mile climb gaining 3,000+ ft. all starting at 8,000 ft. of elevation!
Techno Factor:	(10) Tough, fun singletrack with rocks and obstacles
Fear Factor:	(10) Double skull & crossbones singletrack descent
Route Finding:	A little tough. Experienced riders should be okay.
Season:	Summer/Fall. This is where locals ride in those oh-so-hot summer months. Check with one of the local bike shops before you ride.

Description: This is more like an adventure than a trail ride. A horrible climb on gravel, "Shackleton Expedition" type hike-a-bike at 10,000 ft., and vicious rocky descents, all with scenic views of Canyonlands, creeks, and Aspen forests. Throw in wild flowers, deer, elk, and everything else you'd expect in a Hobbit forest, and call it a "trail" – ha, ha! Start at 8,000 ft. and climb for 8 miles to Geyser Pass. Feeling it yet? Take the double track LEFT (avoiding the 2nd left which happens almost immediately) and descend briefly over RUFF, cobbled 2-track for about a mile. Turn LEFT on the eroded 2-track (note the small FS 240 sign) and head towards Burro Pass (at the saddle between two peaks). After about 1½ brutal miles (much of which must be walked) you reach the pass at 11,600 ft. Now the fun begins! Carefully descend the double skull & crossbones singletrack down from Burro for 2 miles to the signed Mill Creek Trail. Go LEFT. Hammer down Mill Creek till your fillings come loose. After several creek crossings, pick up the trail along side the white water pipes and follow this past a wooden fence to a clearing (about 3 miles). Head straight towards the wooden post (and singletrack) for more stellar riding through Aspen forest. This trail is called both Schuman

and/or Shafer Trail – I know, but don't blame me!
I dare you to find more nasty, wild singletrack anywhere. This
section is loaded with logs, roots, rocks and a few man-made
obstacles sure to excite even the most psychotic Canadian
nutball. Take a RIGHT on Oowah Lake Rd. and a LEFT on the
La Sal Mountain Loop Rd. for a 2 mile ride back to the Geyser
Pass Trailhead and your vehicle.

Options: The more intelligent psycho may want to shuttle up
to Geyser pass to avoid a nasty 8 mile climb on gravel road.
Call a shuttle service or use two vehicles and leave one at the
trail tail.

Directions: From Moab, head SOUTH on Hwy 191 for about 8
miles to the La Sal Mountain Loop Rd. Turn LEFT. At the T-
junction (after ½ mile) turn RIGHT and follow for approx. 12
more miles to signed Geyser Pass Rd. Turn RIGHT onto Geyser
Pass Rd. and park in the pull-out to the left.

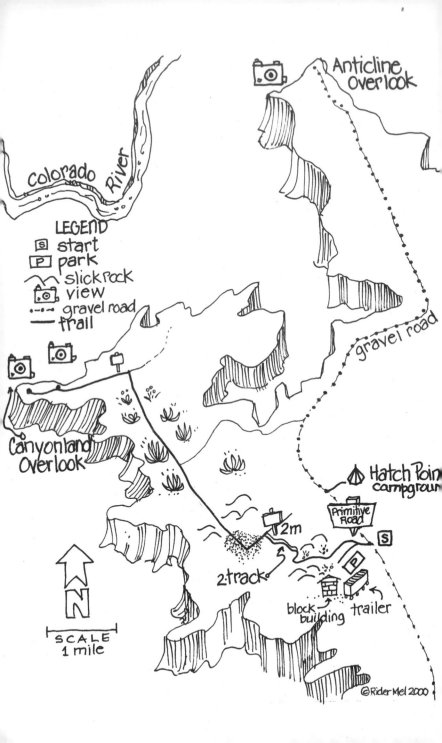

Canyonlands Overlook

scenic intermediate / novice ride

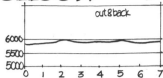

out&back
6000
5500
5000
0 1 2 3 4 5 6 7

Distance: 14 Miles out and back
Time Required: 2 to 3 hours
Grunt Factor: (4) Moderate distance, some sand & ledgy rock
Techno Factor: (3) Nothing tough but a little sand & slickrock
Fear Factor: (3) Nothing scary here other than the overlooks.
Route Finding: Pretty easy, watch for the signs & cairns on rock
Season: Best spring/fall. Start at dawn in summer.

Description: A pretty easy ride with a little distance and amazing views. Take the signed turnoff (Primitive Road) and go past the first spur RIGHT (Trail head) to the parking area beside the block building and tractor-trailer. Now backtrack to the Trailhead and follow the doubletrack for a little under a mile to the slickrock. Just follow the cairns and have fun! As the slickrock ends, look for the 2-track and head across the sandy meadow. Follow the signed turn LEFT at the T-junction through some minor sand to some more slickrock. Around mile 5, take a LEFT at the T-junction and follow the signs to the Overlook. Keep your eyes peeled for photo opp's along the way. On your return be sure to watch for the turns. Strap ole' Bessie on the roof rack and drive up to the Anticline Overlook and more stellar views.

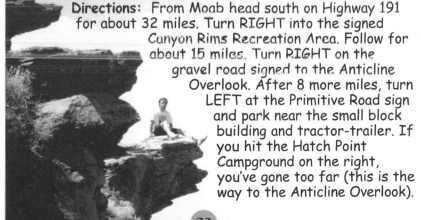

Directions: From Moab head south on Highway 191 for about 32 miles. Turn RIGHT into the signed Canyon Rims Recreation Area. Follow for about 15 miles. Turn RIGHT on the gravel road signed to the Anticline Overlook. After 8 more miles, turn LEFT at the Primitive Road sign and park near the small block building and tractor-trailer. If you hit the Hatch Point Campground on the right, you've gone too far (this is the way to the Anticline Overlook).

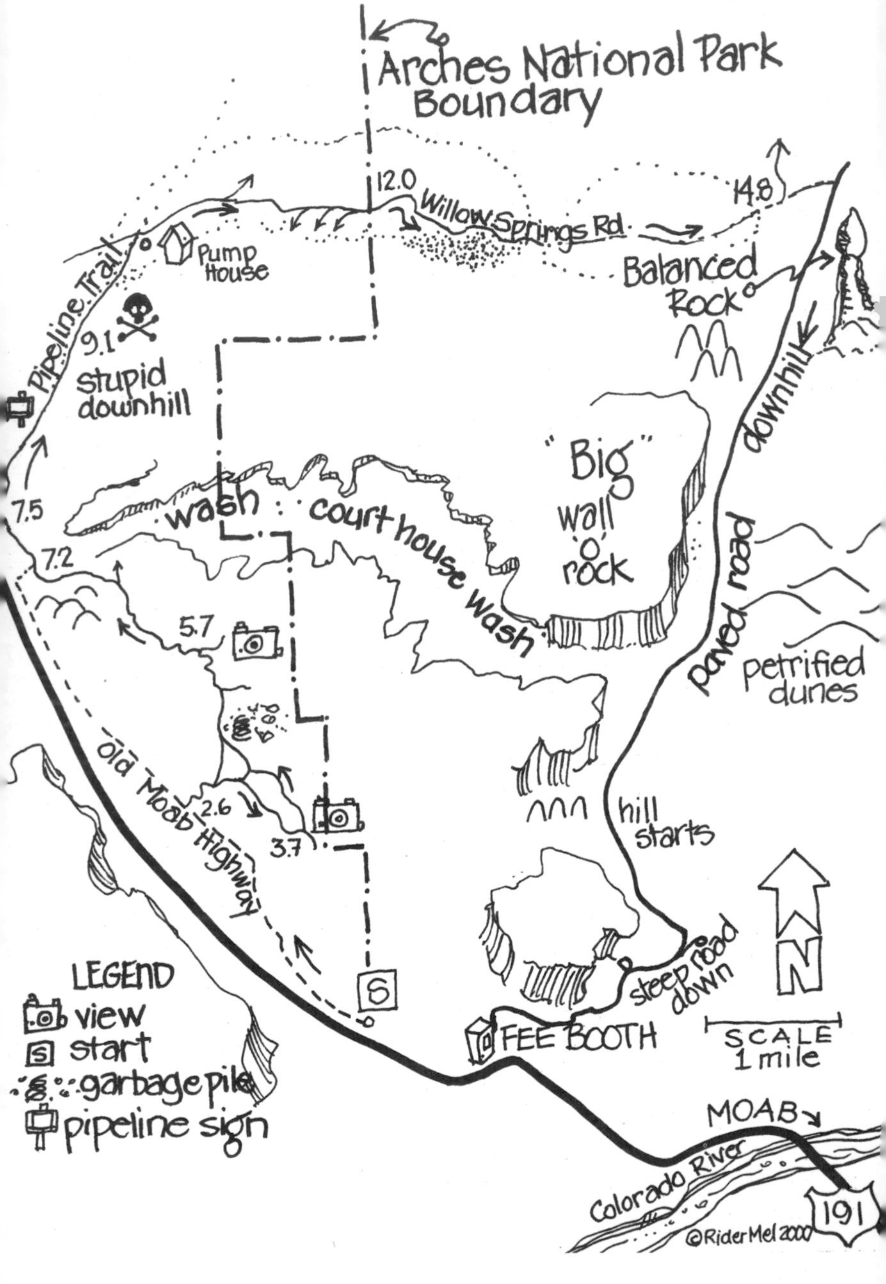

Arches National Park Boundary

Willow Springs Rd 14.8

12.0

Pipeline Trail

Pump House

9.1 stupid downhill

7.5

7.2

wash   court house wash

Balanced Rock

"Big" wall 'o' rock

paved road   downhill

petrified dunes

5.7

2.6
3.7

old Moab Highway

hill starts

6

steep road down

LEGEND
📷 view
⑤ start
·⚐·:· garbage pile
🏮 pipeline sign

FEE BOOTH

SCALE
1 mile

N

MOAB

Colorado River

191

©Rider Mel 2000

Court House Loop

kinda tough, SCENIC!

		loop		

Distance: 26 Mile Loop
Time Required: 3 - 6 Hours
Grunt Factor: (7) Big mileage and some sand
Techno Factor: (4) Mostly easy, some sand and one "stupid" downhill
Fear Factor: (3) Walk the downhill & the scariest part is the road in Arches
Route Finding: Pretty Easy, a few key turns near the beginning
Season: Spring/Fall. Hotter than hell in summer. Bring more water than you can ever imagine you'll need!

Description: See Arches by bike! This route is great for intermediate riders who don't mind a little mileage. You start by riding the old Moab Highway. After about 2½ miles the road turns to dirt. Turn RIGHT at the first spur and climb briefly. Go RIGHT at each of the next two Y-junctions (you will be staying on the "main" route this way). At just under 4 miles take the LEFT turn that almost turns you back around. You'll now be heading North again. Check out the viewpoint into Arches on your right! Follow the Jeep road past the first spur (to the left). Just after the pile of burned out garbage, take the spur RIGHT. From here, simply follow the main route, sticking close to the hill on your left. You'll see lots of tempting slickrock on the right. Play if you like – you remember fun, don't you? You're supposed to enjoy it! Just before the 6 mile point there is a nice photo opp. As you reach the sandy (and rocky) wash, scramble briefly to find the Pipeline Trail off to your left (Northwest). Turn RIGHT and follow the rollers for about 2 miles. You can see Highway 191 and the Archview Campground off to the Northwest. Stay on the Pipeline Trail all the way to Willow Springs Rd. Just before the 10 mile point, the Pipeline Trail becomes a sandy downhill. Walk your bike down the hill (or ride if you like – I believe in Natural Selection). When you reach the wash bottom go right briefly and pick up the trail again at the small concrete pad. You are heading straight towards a pumphouse - you've probably

Court House Loop
—— continued ——

already heard it! Turn RIGHT at Willow Springs Rd. Follow this "main" route for nearly 2 miles. Go LEFT to avoid climbing a steep hill. You'll soon see the Arches Nat'l Park signs – you be in Arches now mang. Follow the "main" trail for about 4 miles through some sand and rock. Did you remember to put on sunscreen? Turn RIGHT at Arches Rd. Follow the pavement for about 10 miles (mostly downhill) to the Park entrance. Enjoy the views of Balanced Rock, The Great Wall, Petrified Dunes, Tower of Babel, Park Avenue and the Three Penguins. You'll have to pay $5 at the gate on the way out. Turn RIGHT onto Highway 191 for about a ½ mile to the Trail Head/Tail.

Directions: From Main and Center Streets in Moab, head north on Main (Hwy 191) for about 6 miles. Just past the entrance to Arches National Park, turn RIGHT into the parking area and head up the old Moab Highway.

BANDITOS GRILL

ALL FRESH
NO CANS

467 N. MAIN
MOAB, UT 84532
435-259-3894
FAX 435-259-1195

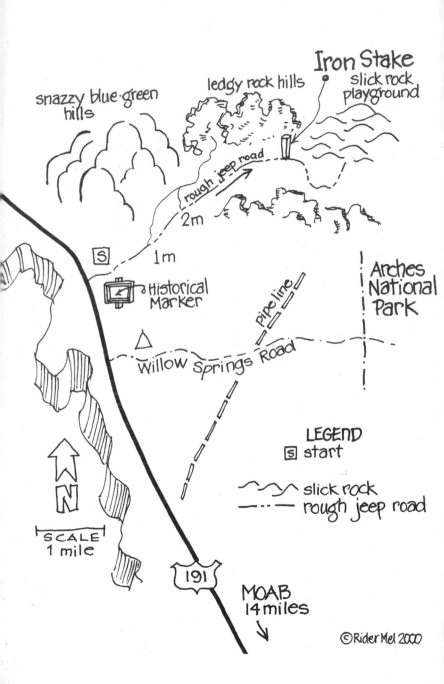

Dalton Wells

slickrock riding for mom and sissy!

Distance: 7 Miles out and back
Time Required: 1 - 2 Hours
Grunt Factor: (2) Short, fun ride with a little sand and easy slickrock
Techno Factor: (2) Nothing tough here
Fear Factor: (2) I get more scared using a microwave!
Route Finding: Pretty easy, you can see the slickrock from the road
Season: Summer is hotter than a snake's ass. Bring as much water as you can carry!

Description: The closest thing to a "Giggle Ride" Moab has to offer. This is a great ride for beginners or those wishing to play around on easy slickrock. Follow the Jeep road from the trail head for 3 miles to the slickrock (you can see it from the trail head). Go RIGHT at the Y-junction at mile 1. Go RIGHT at the Y-junction at mile 2. Basically, you stick to the "main" road and head towards the light-colored slickrock. You'll ride past some snazzy blue-green hills, followed by some ledgy rock hills. A wee climb up to a funny looking iron stake and you're on slickrock. Party like its 1999!

Options: You're on slickrock – do whatever the hell you like. Keep the iron stake in view to avoid slipping into Arches Nat'l Park. Off-roading in National Parks is illegal and would not make your Mom proud.

Directions: From Moab drive north on Highway 191 for about 14 miles. Turn RIGHT at the "Historical Marker" signed turnout. Park and ride!

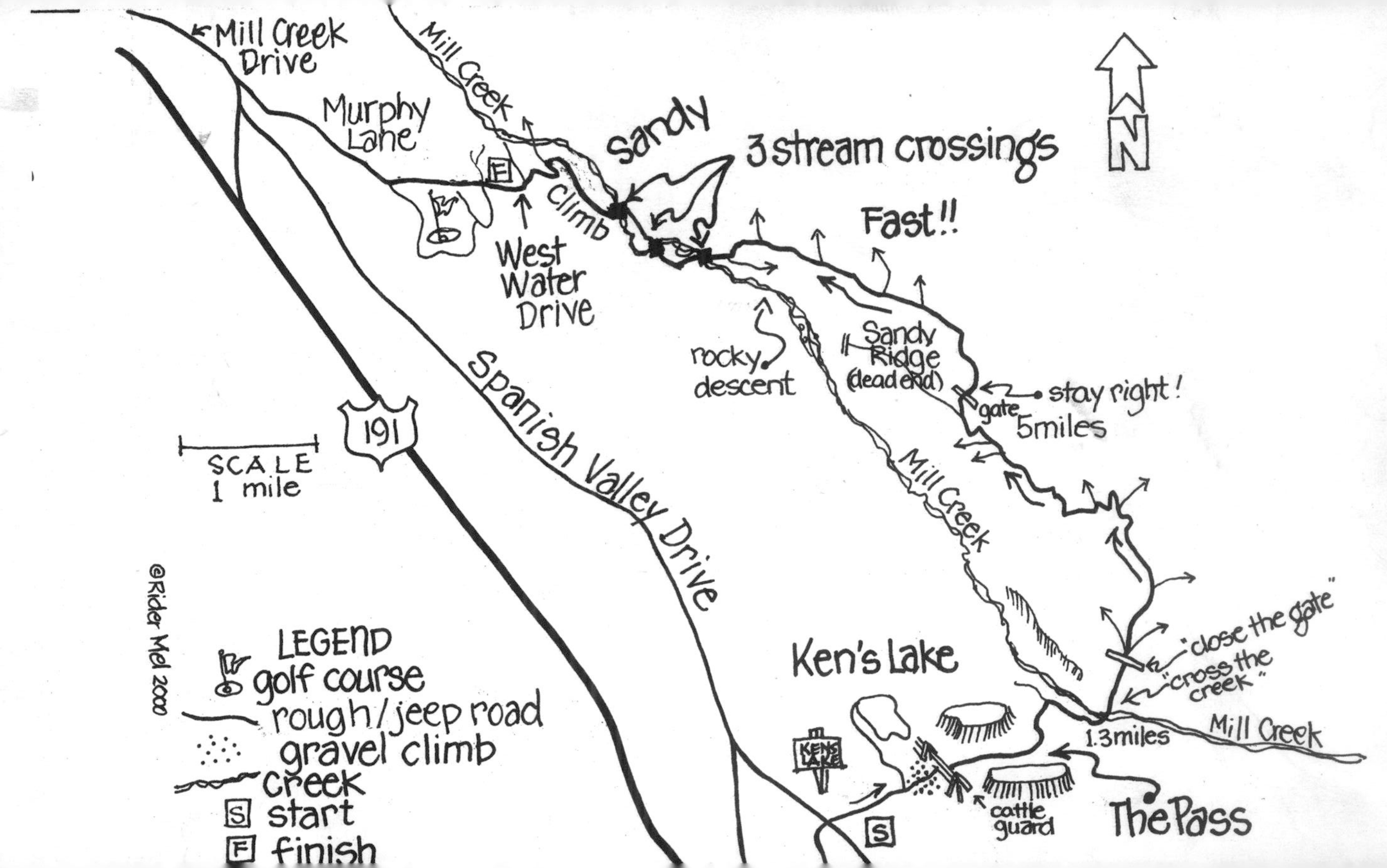

N

3 stream crossings
Fast!!
stay right!
gate 5 miles
Sandy Ridge (dead end)
Sandy
rocky descent
Mill Creek

"close the gate"
"cross the creek"
Mill Creek
.3 miles
The Pass
cattle guard
S

Ken's Lake
KENS

Climb
West Water Drive
E
Murphy Lane
Mill Creek
Mill Creek Drive

Spanish Valley Drive

191

SCALE
1 mile

LEGEND
golf course
rough/jeep road
gravel climb
creek
S start
E finish

©Rider Mel 2000

Flat Pass

tough, classic
Moab riding

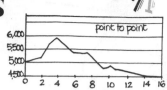

Distance:	16 Miles point to point (including 6 on pavement)
Time Required:	3 to 4 Hours
Grunt Factor:	(8) Difficult, pretty tough rolling trail
Techno Factor:	(9) Difficult, lots of rideable obstacles & lifts
Fear Factor:	(7) Kinda scary in spots, unlikely to leave emotional scars
Route Finding:	Pretty easy, watch for the signs!
Season:	Any, carry mucho water! Start at sunrise in summer!

Description: "Why the heck do they call this FLAT pass anyways?" Okay, so it's not so flat, but it is a cool ride. Lots 'o' rock, plenty of lifts, and even a few stream crossings thrown in – ya, that's right, stream crossings in the desert! The testosterone-charged may want to ride the first crossing, but there's a pretty decent chance you'll get wet. I know some wienies who actually take off their shoes and socks and carry their bikes. No real serious dangers here, but plenty of technical "trouble-balls" which can provide hours of family fun. The last three creek crossings are all easily rideable, but may get your cute little cyclo-sox wet. They're also followed by some annoying sand. No worries, this is mountain biking, not some Eurofag posedown to see who is prettiest and shaves their legs the closest.

Options: This ride can be completed as a loop by riding to the trailhead from town on the route described below. The "ride out" adds about 10 miles of moderate uphill (almost always into a headwind) You can also drive towards the trail head and park along Spanish Valley Drive near the trail tail (see the map) and start your loop. This cuts out most of the road ride from town and eliminates the need for two vehicles.

Directions: From Main x Center, head East on Center. Turn RIGHT on 400 East. Turn LEFT on Mill Creek Drive. Go past Sand Flats Rd. (to Slickrock Trail). After about a mile turn LEFT onto Spanish Valley Drive. Follow for 2 miles and turn

Flat Pass
continued

LEFT at signs for Ken's Lake. Park near Ken's lake and ride up the gravel road climb to the trailhead. Go over the cattle guard and follow the signs (down the hill bear RIGHT, then go LEFT and through the creek).

Logistics: As a point-to-point ride, you either need two cars or a shuttle service. With a shuttle service, you are dropped off at the trailhead and ride back into town. With a "self shuttle" you will need a second vehicle to take back to the trailhead (where you left the first one this morning!)

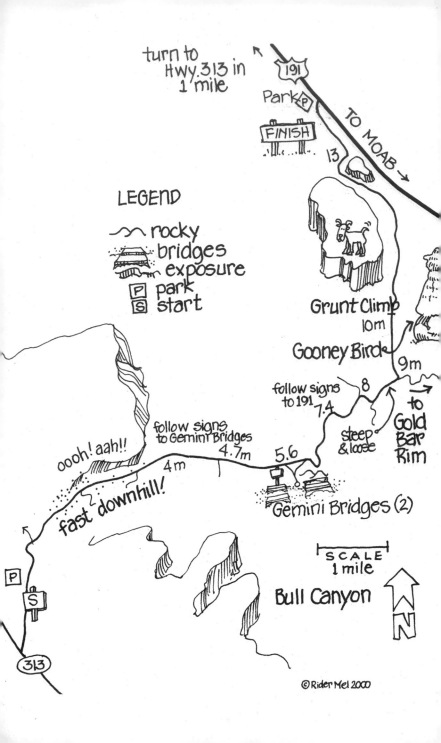

Gemini Bridges

easy, ROCKIN' downhill fun!

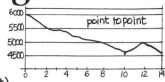

A chart labeled "point to point" showing elevation from 6000 down to 4500 over distance 0 to 14.

Distance: 14 Miles (point to point)

Time Required: 2+ Hours (including time for photos)

Grunt Factor: (3) Almost entirely downhill with one tough climb

Techno Factor: (3) Easy jeep road with optional challenges

Fear Factor: (4) Fast downhill on jeep road – no worries!

Route Finding: Signed the whole way – if you get lost see a doctor.

Season: Any, but hotter than a snake's ass in summer. Ride early, bring water!

Description: This trail is a huge pile of fun. I have a strong dislike for shuttled downhill rides, but I still have to recommend this one. Very fast and simple descent down well signed Jeep road to the Bridges. You can bring your "good" camera on this ride – little chance of crashing. You'll want to spend a little time at the Bridges to take some photos and get scared near the edge. Then just follow the signs to Highway 191 to make your way out. Enough little ledges to keep the strong riders interested, but pretty easy overall. One tough climb at mile 10 followed by another downhill to the trail tail.

Directions: To Trail Head from town, head north on Main (Highway 191) for about 12 miles to Highway 313. Turn LEFT and follow 313 towards the Island in the Sky Recreation Area and Dead Horse Point. Just after mile marker 10 (13 miles after the turn onto 313) turn LEFT at the Gemini Bridges Trail head sign.

Logistics: You'll either need to set up your own shuttle (ie with two cars) or hire a shuttle in town. If you're shuttling yourself, drive both vehicles out of town to the North. At the 11 mile point (before the turn off for Highway 313) there is a turn off to the LEFT with a large parking area. This is the Trail Tail and the spot to leave the shuttle vehicle. Or, if you're using a shuttle service, have them pick you up here so you can drive yourself back into town.

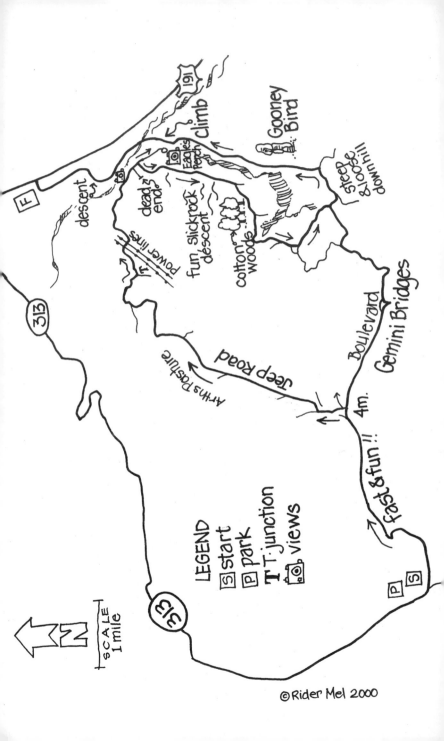

Gemini - Eagle's Perch

point to point

Distance:	22 Miles (point to point)
Time Required:	3 - 5 Hours
Grunt Factor:	(8) Tough, mileage, some climbing, a little sand
Techno Factor:	(7) Tough, rocky climbs, really rocky descent
Fear Factor:	(7) A little scary in spots on descent – nothing to kill you
Route Finding:	Kinda tough! A few key turns, some navigating on rock
Season:	Spring/Fall are best. Hot in summer. Bring mega water.

Description: Little Canyon Rim and Eagle's Perch provide some exceptional views (even by Moab standards)! This is done as a point to point ride using the same trail head and tail as the Gemini Bridges trail. The point to point is a 1,500 ft. descent with a few climbs thrown in. Starting at the Gemini trail head off Hwy 313, head down the wide, gravelly "Boulevard" trail. At the 4 mile point, take the 2-track spur to the far LEFT (see the map). Follow this for just under ½ mile and turn RIGHT on the 2-track spur. Follow this over mild sandy and rocky sections for about 5 miles, avoiding all spurs. Around mile 7, you can see Hwy 313 off to the northwest. You should also be able to see the 2-track trail heading up towards the rim (northeast). At the T-junction turn LEFT and proceed up the hill, going under the power lines. Continue the rocky climb up to the overlooks (you're riding along the rim at this point)! Ooooooowaaaaaaahl If you look really hard, you can see your car in the tiny parking lot along Hwy 191 below. Take some photos and keep riding past two spurs on the right all the way to the Eagle's Perch viewpoint into Little Canyon. The 2-track hits some slickrock and is then marked by rock cairns. When you're done oogling, turn around and backtrack toward the main trail. Turn LEFT on the first spur (to rejoin the main trail, an obvious jeep road which turns to slickrock very quickly). Note: there are two spurs here – make sure you are on the right one – see the map. Follow the rocky descent using tire marks on sand and rock as your guides. Ride through the "Gulch" down the slickrock playground watching for cairns. Basically, you want to follow the "main" route. Keep the rim to your left and take your time and you'll eventually find your way. At around the 13½ mile point (mileages are really ludicrous here), the "main" route will take a RIGHT turn (if you miss this you'll simply reach the rim and have to backtrack). Follow this route down into a wash (with the potential for a quick swim where you see the Cottonwood trees) and back up the other side to the left. At around the 15 mile point, take the LEFT turn onto a 2-track over hard sand and slickrock (if you miss this turn you'll reach the Boulevard and the way out anyways). Once you reach the Boulevard (that wide gravel road you started on) turn LEFT and follow the signs to Hwy 191.

Options: Make this a fun, technical, out and back ride and eliminate much of the initial sandy 2-track through "Arths Pasture". See the Little Canyon Rim description/map.

Directions: To Trail Head from town, head north on Main (Highway 191) for about 12 miles to Highway 313. Turn LEFT and follow 313 towards the Island in the Sky Recreation Area and Dead Horse Point. Just after mile marker 10 (13 miles after the turn onto 313) turn LEFT at the Gemini Bridges Trail head sign.

Logistics: You'll either need to set up your own shuttle (ie with two cars) or hire a shuttle in town. If you're shuttling yourself, drive both vehicles out of town to the North. At the 11 mile point (before the turn off for Highway 313) there is a turn off to the LEFT with a large parking area. This is the Trail Tail and the spot to leave the shuttle vehicle. Or, if you're using a shuttle service, have them pick you up here so you can drive yourself back into town.

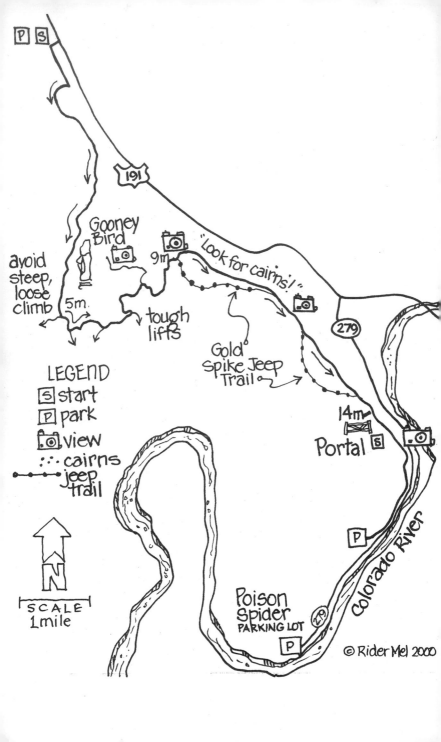

Gold Bar Rim

Moab's "Moses Ride"

point to point

Distance: 16 Miles (Point to point
                       using Portal Trail)
Time Required: 4 - 6 Hours
Grunt Factor: (10) Tough, lots of lifts
Techno Factor: (10) Tough, rocky climbs, Portal descent
Fear Factor: (8) Sometimes scary near the "rim", Portal = 11
Route Finding: Good luck! Easy at first. Once onto the rim
                       look for cairns and have fun – losing the trail
                       (at least briefly) is a near certainty.

Description: Gold Bar Rim is one of those infamous
trails – real lunatics and experts need to do it at
least once. Don't let the mileage fool you – this one
is a "Moses ride" (ie you wander around the desert
for about 40 years). You start with a climb on jeep
road, followed by a little bit of sandy going. At last
you hit the rocky stuff and lifts, lifts, lifts. If
you don't like little technical maneuvers you may
want to pass on this trail. Once you reach the
rim the strategy is pretty simple: follow the cairns (if you can
find them) and when in doubt stay as close to the rim as you
can. The Gold Spike jeep trail (marked by spray painted spikes)
follows the same route for much of the way, but departs to the
South (right, away from the rim, what else can I tell you?)
several times. Eventually you reach a T-junction. Go LEFT to
meet up with the Portal Trail and some scenic, scary, hike-a-
biking. Or, go RIGHT to descend the Poison Spider Mesa trail,
over slickrock and sand, adding 6 miles to your total.

Options: As mentioned, the route can be done point to point
using either the Portal Trail or the Poison Spider Mesa trail. For
my money take the Portal, enjoy the views and ride only where it
is safe (relatively) to do so.

Logistics: You'll need to use a shuttle service for this ride or
set up your own shuttle with two cars. Either way, you need to
leave a vehicle on Hwy 279 (Potash Rd.) at the trail tail of your
choice. The options are: the Lion's Park campground just past
the Portal trail tail if you are using the Portal option, or the
Poison Spider Mesa parking area a few miles further down the
road (marked with the "Dinosaur Tracks" sign).

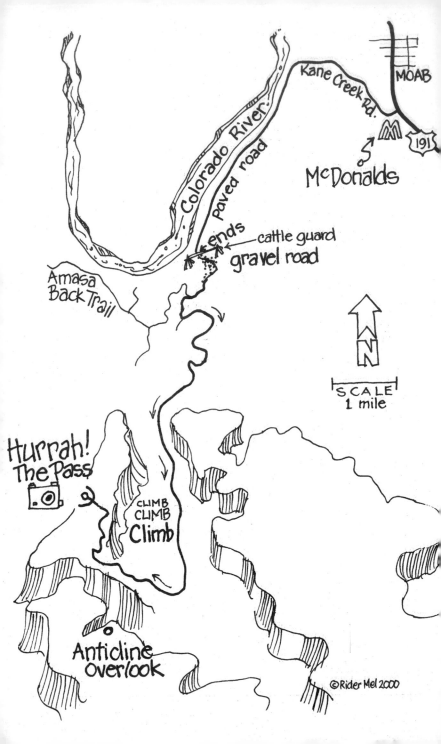

Hurrah Pass

big miles, not too tough!

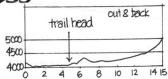

Distance: 20 Miles out and back (or 30 miles riding from town)

Time Required: 2 - 5 Hours

Grunt Factor: (6) A long climb on gravel, steep near the Pass

Techno Factor: (3) Easy, need to control your speed on descent

Fear Factor: (4) Only thing to fear is excess speed on descent

Route Finding: Dead easy. More chance of getting lost in frozen food section at City Market.

Season: Best spring/fall. Start at sunrise in the summer.

Description: Ideal for those who love to toil, this is essentially a grunt along a gravelly road up to the Pass. You are rewarded with some nice canyon scenery and a great view from the pass. Bring water and food! Kinda reminds me of road biking without the road bike, but be my guest. Along the way, you'll pass the Amasa Back trailhead (around mile 1.5). At the top you'll be looking down into the Colorado River Gorge and the Moab Spring Race course (listed as a separate ride).

Options: This is a simple out-and-back ride. As such, you can turn around at any point and retrace your steps back. The climb up to Hurrah Pass over the last 3 miles is the toughest part (but rewards you with the view and the downhill back).

Directions: Either ride from town to maximize your mileage (at about 30 miles) or drive up to the Kane Creek Campground. From Main x Center head SOUTH on Main (HWY 191). Turn RIGHT at McDonalds onto Kane Creek Rd. Stay on Kane Creek past the Scenic Chairlift and around the curve. Go past the Moab Rim trailhead parking lot on your left. Park in the lot just before the cattle gate (where the pavement ends). Ride up the gravel road and enjoy.

Klondike Bluffs

big fun
intermediate ride

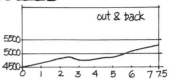

out & back

5500
5000
4500
0 1 2 3 4 5 6 7 7.5

Distance: 15 Miles out and back
Time Required: 3 Hours (including time for hike and photos)
Grunt Factor: (4) Fairly easy climb with a few tough spots
Techno Factor: (3) Mostly easy with a few "fun spots" on slickrock
Fear Factor: (3) Nothing to scare you. Bring the wife and kids if they can handle a moderate climb for 7 miles
Route Finding: Easy, watch for cairns & paint dashes on slickrock
Season: Any, but HOT in the summer. Bring Lotsa Water!

Description: This is one of the best Intermediate/Novice trails in Moab. It starts with an easy (but fairly long) climb. A nice mix of Jeep Road and Slickrock with a couple of short sandy sections. Also a short hike at the end to some tremendous views. Stop and rest in the "Flintstone" residence at mile 4. Check out the Dinosaur Tracks (circled with rocks) near the start of the Slickrock. Just before the 8 mile point, the bike trail ends. Check out the abandoned mine shaft up to the RIGHT. Be Careful! Leave your bike (you may want to lock it) and hike up to the overlook. Upon return, find a bike you like (remember, fit is important, not just color scheme and Brand) and cruise the downhill back to the Trail head. Play on the Slickrock if you like. It's okay, even your Mom would approve of this place. Newcomers may want to practice some "lifts" or steeps to prepare themselves for other more severe trails.

Directions: From Main and Center in Moab, take Highway 191 North for 17 miles. Pull into the turnoff RIGHT just after mile marker 142 and follow the signs – easy as pie!

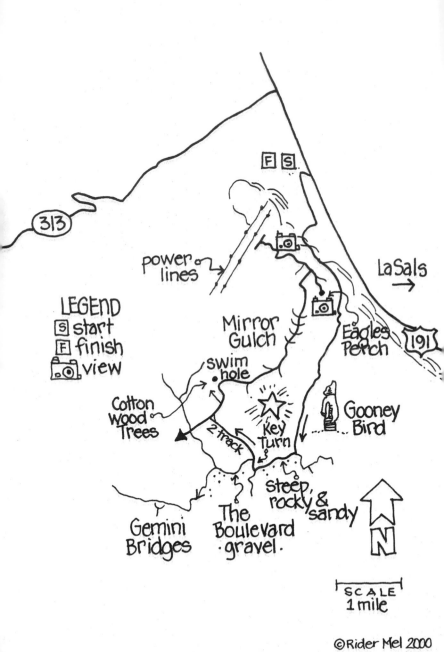

313

F S

power lines

LaSals →

LEGEND
S start
F finish
📷 view

Mirror Gulch

Eagles Perch

191

swim hole

Cotton wood Trees

2 track

Key Turn

Gooney Bird

steep, rocky & sandy

Gemini Bridges

The Boulevard gravel.

N

SCALE
1 mile

©Rider Mel 2000

Little Canyon Rim

out & back

Distance: 22 Miles (out and back)
Time Required: 4 - 6 Hours
Grunt Factor: (10) Tough, mileage & climbing
Techno Factor: (9) Tough slickrock climb/descent, the "Gulch"
Fear Factor: (7) A little scary in spots
Route Finding: Kinda tough. A few key turns, some navigating on rock
Season: Spring/Fall are best. Hot in the summer.

Description: This is the "I don't use no damn shuttle" alternative to the Gemini – Eagle's Perch ride described separately. The same mileage, but don't be fooled – this one starts 1,000 ft. lower and climbs (mostly) for 11 miles! No worries – climbing on slickrock is more fun than ... okay, I won't go that far, but it's REALLY fun. From the trail head off Highway 191, climb the hill and go up the steep, loose climb (signed to Gemini Bridges) just before the 5 mile point. Avoid the spur on the left to Bull Canyon and take the next spur RIGHT. Now just follow the 2-track, turning RIGHT at the T-junction. Follow the trail down into a wash with Cottonwoods and back up the other side. As you reach the slickrock, look for the "traveled route" and cairns. Keep the rim to your right and your eyes open. This slickrock route provides fun challenges and your fair share of laughs if you visualize jeepers trying to maneuver through it all. Once you reach the top (hard to miss) go RIGHT to Eagle's Perch then backtrack to the rim. Try to spot your car in the parking lot waaaaaaaayy down there to the left! Then simply return the way you came.

Options: This can be done as a point to point with a lot less climbing utilizing both the Gemini Bridges trail head and tail. See separate trail description and map under Gemini – Eagle's Perch.

Directions: To Trail Head from town, head north on Main (Highway 191) for about 11 miles to a large parking area on the LEFT. This is the Gemini Bridges Trail Tail and the spot to park.

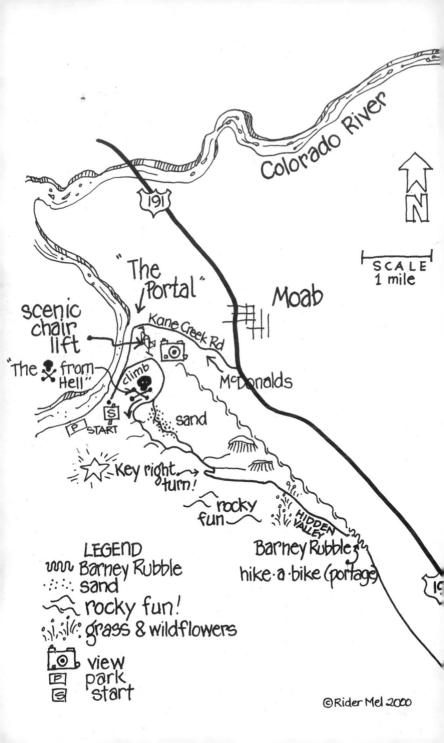

Moab Rim

masochist's dreamride!

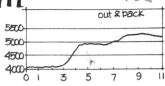

out & back

	5500						
	5000						
	4500						
	4000						
0	1	3	5	7	9	11

Distance: 22 Miles out and back (including 6 on pavement)

Time Required: 3 to 4 Hours

Grunt Factor: (11) Difficult, unbelievably tough climb, o/w Rolling Fun

Techno Factor: (8) Difficult, steep climb/descent with techno moves

Fear Factor: (7) Some scary spots on climb, (11) on descent!

Route Finding: Easy

Season: Any, carry water! Summer = ride at crack of dawn!

Description: This trail has the nastiest 1 mile of climbing imaginable. Downhiller? Big ass? Just hate to climb? Take the chairlift! They used to hold a race from river to rim every year at the Moab Fat Tire Festival. The winning times were around 12 minutes – about the same time you and I spend leaning over our handlebars trying to hold down breakfast. Don't fret, almost all the hard work is in that first mile. Then it's up and down fun tracing through big patches of slickrock and jeep trail. Some petroglyphs to be found here too! At the end of the meadow (I know, I know, but I swear it IS a desert) turn around and get ready for a ROCKIN return. You can easily be back in town sippin on a Café Americano within one hour of the turn around – wish the climb was that easy.

Route Finding Key Spots: Follow the signs. Around the 7 mile mark follow the Jeep road straight to the Hidden Valley Trail. Keep the large Butte (with petroglyphs) on your left. A short ways up, take the spur to the right to reach the rocky, technical section and Hidden Valley.

Moab Rim
continued

Options: Many people suggest riding this one as a loop from town. You can climb up from the river as I suggest and instead of turning around, take the hike-a-bike (called Barney Rubble by locals) down to the valley and ride the road back into town. You can also start with the hike-a-bike and ride back to the river, turning the wicked climb into a heinous technical descent. Okay, so you wanna downhill? Buy a pass on the Scenic Chairlift and knock yourself out.

Directions: From Main x Center head SOUTH on HWY 191. Turn RIGHT at McDonalds onto Kane Creek Rd. Stay on Kane Creek past the Scenic Chairlift and around the curve. Look for the trailhead parking lot on your left.

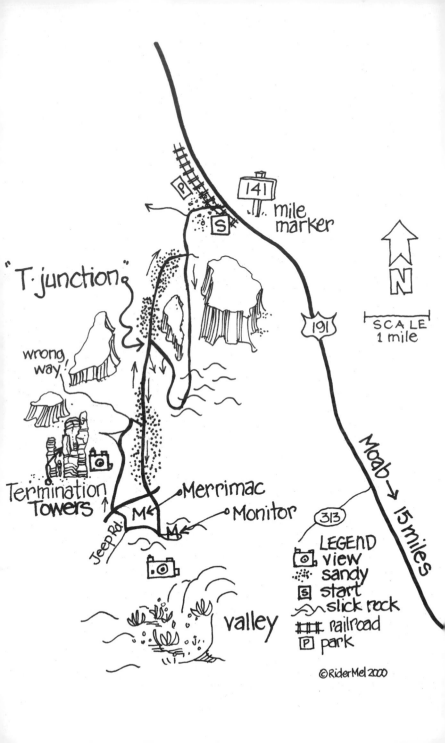

"T·junction"

wrong way

Termination Towers

Jeep Rd.

Merrimac

Monitor

valley

mile marker

141

191

313

Moab → 15 miles

LEGEND
view
sandy
start
slick rock
railroad
park

©RiderMel 2000

Monitor & Merrimac

kinda tough loops with TV commercial views

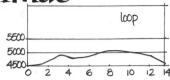

Distance: 14 Mile figure-eight Loop

Time Required: 2 - 5 Hours

Grunt Factor: (5) Mostly easy with about 2 miles of tough sandy going

Techno Factor: (4) Mostly easy, some sand and a slickrock playground

Fear Factor: (4) Slickrock behind Merrimac is a little steep in spots

Route Finding: First loop is easy. You need to look for a 2-track road off the slickrock behind Merrimac. A little confusing around Termination Towers.

Season: Spring/Fall. In summer ride early and bring tons of water.

Description: This is a GREAT scenic ride. The "price-tag" is some riding through nasty sand. From the parking lot, follow the jeep road and take a LEFT turn at the sign for "Mill Canyon". You'll pass the old Stagecoach Halfway Station on your right. Just past the 2½ mile point, jump onto the slickrock and follow the painted lines. Follow the markers around the butte clockwise on a mild downhill. Go through the wash to the T-junction and bear LEFT. (To shorten this ride and/or avoid much of the sand you can turn around and backtrack or turn RIGHT at the T-junction and endure only a little sand.) The trail from the junction point out to Monitor (almost 2 miles) is pretty sandy. For best results, maintain your speed, keep your weight back and spin the pedals quickly. Note, this is also a pretty effective way to get REALLY tired! Be prepared to walk some of the sandier sections. As you approach the Monitor and Merrimac Buttes (at around the 5½ mile point, take the 2nd spur on the left (it pretty much heads towards the slickrock). Once on the rock, follow the base around to the LEFT. The routefinding here is a little "free-form", but easy as long as you keep Monitor on your right. Once around the back you can marvel at the canyon/bowl and take some photos. Then just follow the base around (keeping the butte on your right) to the slickrock playground behind

Monitor & Merrimac
continued

Merrimac. Follow the "off camber" slickrock around the base of Merrimac and keep your eyes peeled for a 2-track jeep road. This can be a little tricky, but you shouldn't get too lost if you use the map, some overall orientation and your gray matter. Turn RIGHT onto the jeep road and roll northward towards Termination Towers (TV commercial heaven!). After playing around the Towers, get back on the jeep road and head North (or LEFT for those with a pathetic sense of direction) all the way up to the trailhead. You'll pass the Mill Canyon Dinosaur Trail on your left. At the junction (where you turned left to start the trail) go LEFT to reach the parking lot.

Options: This trail is scenic and fun, but can be vicious for those who hate sand. You can 1) back track after the 5 mile point and the first slickrock cowpie when you reach the T-junction 2) bypass the second loop in the figure-8 and simply complete the first loop by turning RIGHT at the T-junction. This option entails some sand and some nice views.

Directions: From town, drive North on Highway 191 for about 15 miles. Just past mile marker 141, turn LEFT on the dirt road and proceed over the railway tracks to the parking area on the right. Saddle up and ride down the road to the signed LEFT turn to the Monitor and Merrimac Trail.

"Who brought the Perrier and Hummus?"

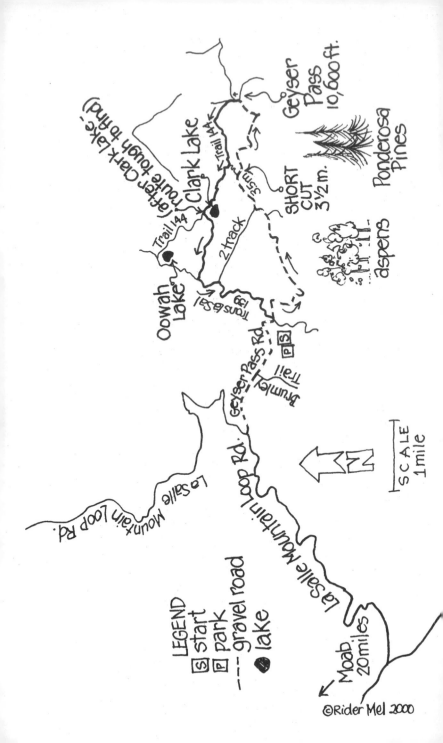

Moonlight Meadow

tough, beautiful
singletrack in the mountains

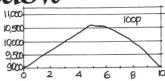

Distance:	10 mile loop
Time Required:	2 - 3 Hours
Grunt Factor:	(7) Five mile climb at altitude, tough fun singletrack
Techno Factor:	(8) Rocky, rooty, un-maintained 1-track
Fear Factor:	(7) Some mild exposure and steep bits, lotsa rocky dirt trail
Route Finding:	Kinda tough. Two key turns.
Season:	Summer/Fall but NOT after rainfall.

Description: Don't take the name too literally – moonlight alone is inadequate to safely ride this trail – I'm serious! Moonlight Meadow offers some exceptionally fun, tough singletrack riding. Climb Geyser Pass Rd. 5 miles to the Pass (elev. 10,500 ft.). Take the spur LEFT and turn LEFT again almost immediately onto a less traveled 2-track trail (Trail 144). As the pasture opens up, pick up the singletrack on the left and party down the rocky route. After about 1½ miles, you will pass a spur to the left (which leads back to Geyser Pass Rd.). Continue straight ahead through mud, creeks, and fallen trees for just under 1 mile. As you approach a small lake (Clark Lake) down the hill on your left, pick up the singletrack descent with a couple of switchbacks. Head around the right side to the back of the lake and pick up the singletrack trail heading straight back to the West. (If you follow the trail along the lake instead, you will find yourself at Oowah Lake in a little over a mile) After 1 mile, the trail reaches a T-junction Turn LEFT (onto the Trans La Sal trail). Stay on the singletrack - avoid the 2-track trail heading left back up to Geyser Pass. Cross logs, rocks, cows and a creek till you reach the trail head at Geyser Pass Rd (and your vehicle).

Directions: From Moab, head SOUTH on Hwy 191 for about 8 miles to the La Sal Mountain Loop Rd. Turn LEFT. At the T-junction (after ½ mile) turn RIGHT. Follow this road for approx. 12 more miles to the signed Geyser Pass Rd. Turn RIGHT and follow the gravel road for just under 3 miles to the signed Trans La Sal trail junction (where the road curves left) and park in the pull-out to the right. Now just saddle up and start pedaling up the gravel road (see the map).

F 4,200 ft.
128
Creek Crossings
Fisher Valley Road
NARROWS 19m
Cottonwood Canyon Trail
GRUNT
8m
Hideout Campsite
15m
Fisher Valley Rd.
NASTY CLIMB
Thompson Canyon Trail
7,500 ft.
Polar Mesa Trail
spur
1m
Bull Draw Campsite
North Beaver Mesa
8,000' S
LEGEND
S start
F finish
higher elevation
viewpoint
SCALE
1 mile
Castle Valley Road
N
© Rider Mel 2000

North Beaver Mesa to Onion Creek

aspens to sagebrush descent

Distance: 26 Miles Point to Point
Time Required: 3 - 5 Hours
Grunt Factor: (6) A long, fast downhill with one tough climb
Techno Factor: (5) Rough descent in spots, mostly easy
Fear Factor: (5) Just some speed and minor exposure
Route Finding: Easy. Well signed and easy to follow.
Season: Spring/Summer(Early morning)/Fall.

Description: Like to Downhill? This one's for you. A 26 mile descent of nearly 4,000 feet with very little climbing! Oh ya, throw in about 20 creek crossings near the bottom and some absolutely KILLER views. Disclaimer: the water in Onion Creek is extremely salty (and corrosive). Those who sleep with their bikes may want to avoid this one altogether. Otherwise, wash your bike completely after the ride. Oh ya, you'll need two vehicles or one of the local shuttle services. Why ride it, you ask? FOUR THOUSAND FOOT descent with great photo opps! Use the map and follow the signs: N. Beaver Mesa LEFT on Thompson Canyon Trail, RIGHT at junction after nasty climb, LEFT at junction of Fisher Valley and Cottonwood Canyon Trails.

Logistics: From Main and Center streets in town, drive north on Main (Hwy 191) to Highway 128 where the Colorado River cuts into the Canyon. Turn RIGHT on Hwy 128 and proceed for about 20 miles past the signed road into Castle Valley (this is the road you will take up to the trailhead). Take the signed "Campground" turnout after the "Onion Creek" sign (at approx. mile 20 from the turn onto Hwy 128). Drive down the gravel road to the signed parking area and drop off the shuttle vehicle. Using the second vehicle, shuttle riders and bikes back SOUTH on Hwy 128 for about 4 miles to the signed road into Castle Valley. Turn LEFT (East) onto Castle Valley Road and follow it for about 19 miles passing the La Sal Mountain Loop Road on the right. The pavement will turn to gravel/dirt. Continue (if you wish) to a three way intersection signed to "N. Beaver Mesa". Saddle up and ride the LEFT spur towards North Beaver Mesa.

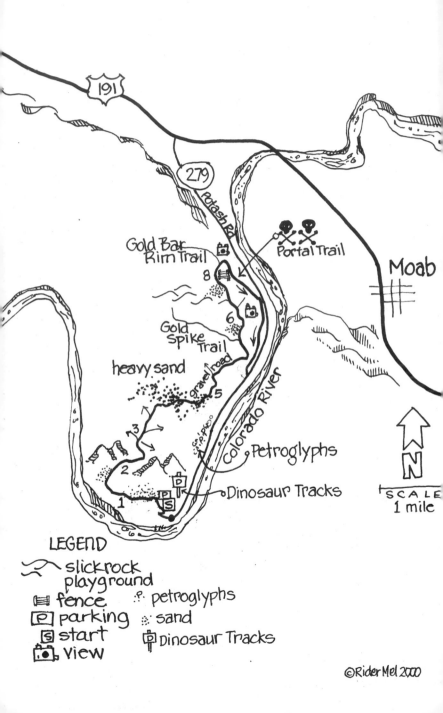

191

279

Potash Rd.

Portal Trail

Moab

Gold Bar
Rim Trail

8

Gold
Spike
Trail

6

heavy sand

gravel road

5

Colorado River

3

Petroglyphs

2

Dinosaur Tracks

1

P
S

N

SCALE
1 mile

LEGEND

slickrock
playground
fence   petroglyphs
parking   sand
start   Dinosaur Tracks
view

©Rider Mel 2000

Poison Spider Mesa

technical playground with fist-clenching sandy spots

turn around point ↓

5000
4500
4000

0 2 4 6 8 10 12 13

Distance: 16 Miles Out-and-back (or 13 Mile Loop with Portal Trail)

Time Required: 3 - 5 Hours

Grunt Factor: (8) Pretty tough climb with lots of sand, some steep ups

Techno Factor: (9) Lots of obstacles, BIG fun

Fear Factor: (7) Nothing too nasty (unless using Portal to close loop!)

Route Finding: Fairly Easy. Watch for signs and painted jeeps on rock.

Season: Spring/Fall are best. Can get extremely sandy in summer (also very hot so ride early and bring a ton of water).

Important: Read the Portal Trail write-up if riding as a loop!

Description: Poison Spider Mesa is jam packed with fun little obstacles and a slickrock playground. It also delivers WAY more than your recommended daily allowance of sand, so be forewarned. Start with a steady, sometimes technical climb to some slickrock and a 2-track through a field. Follow the little painted jeeps on the rock – remember, the spare tire is on the back! If you want to free-form, just keep your bearings and have fun (and forget any mileage counts). Once you make it to the large slickrock cowpie its bikesurf heaven. Some steep ups/downs to play on with even more nasty stuff if you invent your own line (be careful). Following the jeeps will give you a lollipop out-and-back (ie a little loop at the end of the out) and allow you to downhill the climb you made up to the rim. If you are skilled, lobotomized and generally angry you can ride the Portal Trail down to make this a loop. Just after you pass the fence, turn RIGHT to access the Portal Trail or LEFT to head back down Poison Spider. Both the Surgeon General and the BLM do NOT recommend riding the Portal Trail. Read the review of the Portal entirely before considering it!

Options: Are you paying attention? I just told you, the Portal Trail (double skull & crossbones death on the left) will turn

Poison Spider Mesa
— continued —

this into a loop, dropping you (only figuratively I hope) onto Hwy 279 about 2 miles from the trailhead. Along the way you can check out a plethora of petroglyphs (both signed and unsigned).

Directions: From town, drive north on Hwy 191 just past Arches Nat'l Park to Hwy 279 (Potash Rd.) Turn LEFT. Follow this road for about 6 miles to the trailhead signed "Dinosaur Tracks". Park in the gravel lot, use the fancy pit toilets (sure beats trail crapping), and follow the signs to the trail.

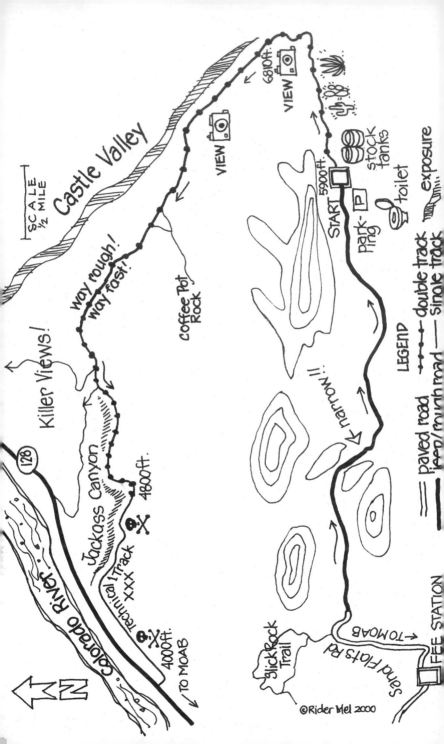

Porcupine Rim

cornucopia of off-road fun

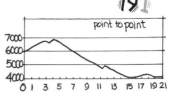

point to point

Distance: 21 Mile Point to Point (or 30 Mile Loop)
Time Required: 3 to 6 Hours
Grunt Factor: (10) Pretty Tough Climb, Teeth Rattling Downhill
Techno Factor: (10) Some skill moves on the climb, lot's 'o' small drops, some techno moves with scary exposure on the singletrack.
Fear Factor: (11) Kinda scary on 2-track downhill, heinous in some spots on singletrack.
Route Finding: Pretty simple - follow the signs & tire tracks
Season: ANY, BUT it's dangerously hot in summer - ride at crack of dawn

Description: This trail has it all – nice climb with some technical moves, unbelievable views and photo opp's, ROCKIN' fast 2-track downhill, and some technical singletrack at the bottom (with Death on The Right!).

Climb for about 4½ miles up from the Stock Tanks. See the map. Or, if you're super fit or super masochistic, ride up from town. It will add about 9 miles and 2,000 ft. of climbing. Break out the Chardonnay and hors d'oeuvres at the top while you enjoy the overlook into Castle Valley. Engage in some intelligent conversation, then hammer down the 2-track like gravity ain't no thang. Lots 'o' drops and rough stuff. Retribution for everyone who spent mega-dollars on a downhill bike that weighs more than the average mother-in-law. Remember, fast is good, and try to keep your skin where it belongs. After the creek bed its up into the singletrack piece de la resistance. There are some pretty scary techno moves here. Don't be afraid to walk them. Ride everything if you like – I believe in natural selection. Finish off with a 6 mile road ride into town (loaded with more "shitty views"), have a beer, and repair your bike for the next ride!

Porcupine Rim
—— continued ——

Option: Downhillers can have the shuttle drop them off about 2 miles further up the Sand Flats Rd. and take the spur (LEFT) to the trail. This makes the climb up to the top a little easier, but you'll need a 4WD or something similar. Hiring a shuttle for this one has its definite advantages!

Directions: From Main x Center streets in town, head EAST on Center. Turn RIGHT on 400 East. Turn LEFT on Mill Creek Drive. Turn LEFT at Sand Flats Rd. and follow it up past the fee station (buy the car pass for $5 – it's good for 3 days!). Go past the Slickrock Trail parking area to where the pavement turns to gravel and follow the road to the Stock Tanks (about 7 miles from the fee station). This road is completely drivable, albeit bumpy. I've done it in a mini-van with two kids in child seats. Puts 'em right to sleep! If you ride from town, you're adding 9 miles and 2,000 feet of climbing.

Portal Trail

death on the left
riding/hiking

Distance: 2 Miles (from Rim to River)
Time Required: 1 Hour or less
Grunt Factor: (4) Trials-type bike handling and/or hike-a-bike
Techno Factor: (11) Big descent, big rocks, BIG danger
Fear Factor: (11) Off the map unless you are blind or brain damaged
Route Finding: Very easy. No real alternative to the trail.
Season: See Poison Spider Mesa or Gold Bar Rim descriptions.

Description: Okay, have you figured it out yet? This trail is simply not safe to ride in its entirety. Many parts of it probably shouldn't give you more than a compound fracture. A couple of pieces, however, have killed in the past – read the signs. If you find yourself on this trail without pondering mortality you are probably the type who wants to ride it all. My heartfelt condolences go out to your relatives – I'm serious. Okay, I'll stop. This trail does allow you to ride either Poison Spider Mesa or the Gold Bar Rim as a loop ride. It also affords some breathtaking views. Just promise yourself you will walk the exposed sections and enjoy. The most difficult technical challenges occur after the most exposed portions of the trail. Downhillers and North Shore types will find this lower portion to be "gnarly sismo burlaceous fun".

Directions: Trailhead can only be accessed by riding up from the Poison Spider Mesa or Gold Bar Rim trails (or hiking UP the Portal T guess). From trail tail (on Hwy 279 near the Colorado River), simply go right on the road and pedal for about 2 miles to the Poison Spider trailhead, or less than a mile to the nearest pullout where you left a shuttle vehicle.

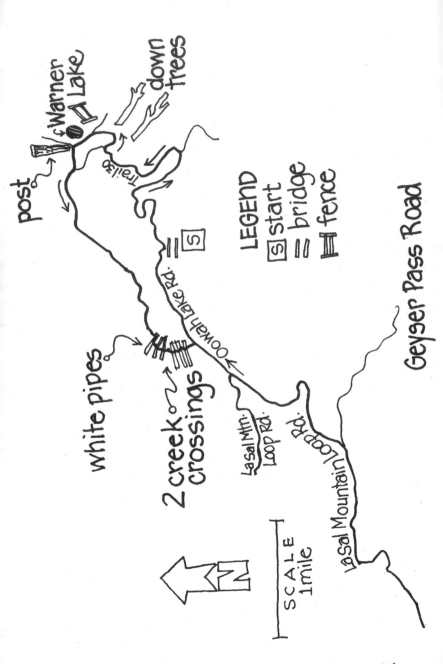

post

Warner Lake

down trees

Trail 30

LEGEND
ⓢ = start
⚏ = bridge
Ⅲ = fence

Owah Lake Rd.

white pipes

2 creek crossings

Lasal Mtn. Loop Rd.

LaSal Mountain Loop Rd.

Geyser Pass Road

N

SCALE 1 mile

©Rider Mel 2000

Schuman's Gulch

wild, fast, fun, technical mountain singletrack

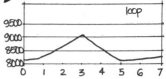

loop

Distance: 7 Miles

Time Required: 1 - 2 Hours

Grunt Factor: (7) Short, gravel road climb at altitude

Techno Factor: (8) Rocky, rooty, fun stuff that can hurt you

Fear Factor: (7) Some mild exposure and steep bits, lotsa rocky dirt trail

Route Finding: Reasonably easy. Only advanced riders should venture into the La Sals.

Season: Summer/Fall but NOT after rainfall. Best to check at a local bike shop first.

Description: Schuman's Gulch is a great "getaway" ride in the heat of summer. This loop is "short & sweet" with a little bit of "tough" thrown in. Park near the bridge (which crosses the creek) on Oowah Lake Rd. and ride up the gravel for a little over a mile. Turn LEFT on Trail 30 and continue climbing (often over fallen trees) up to Warner Lake. Now the real fun begins! Once you pass the fence, look for the wooden post and head straight for it. Fly down the singletrack (only figuratively) over roots, logs, and fallen riders. Go up and over the large white pipes and cross the creek not once, but twice. Hey, shut up, it's my nursery rhyme! Turn LEFT onto Oowah Lake Road and ride up to your car. You may want to try a second lap – the directions are pretty much the same as for the first.

Directions: From Moab, head SOUTH on Hwy 191 for about 8 miles to the La Sal Mountain Loop Rd. Turn LEFT. At the T-junction (after ½ mile) turn RIGHT and follow for approx. 14 more miles to Oowah Lake Rd. Turn RIGHT onto Oowah Lake Rd. and follow for a little over a mile to a bridge crossing the creek. Park and ride up the road.

Slickrock Bike Trail

yyyeah baby!
This is the one you've
read about.

(elevation profile graph showing "loop", with y-axis marks 5000, 4500, 4000 and x-axis 0 through 13)

Distance: Main Loop 13 Miles, Practice Loop 2.5 Miles

Time Required: 2 to 5 Hours

Grunt Factor: (10) Very Tough Roller Coaster Ride – lots 'o' short steeps

Techno Factor: (10) Very Difficult. Very Steep Ups/Downs on ROCK

Fear Factor: (10) Very Scary in spots

Route Finding: Follow the painted white dashes. Dots go to overlooks!

Season: Spring/Fall or EARLY morning in summer. Bring all the water you can – no shade, muy caliente!

Description: Most fun you can have with your clothes on! Drive up from town or ride up and add 2 miles and 1,200 feet of climbing. There is a $2 fee at the Sand Flats Recreation Area booth – believe me, it's worth it! The ride is 13 miles of roller-coaster fun. Unbelievably steep ups (yes, Virginia some people do make all the climbs) and downs – be careful. All of the spurs marked by dots are well worth the effort. The Portal Viewpoint provides exceptional photo opp's. The Main Loop is marked with an "Easy" and a "Hard" way. They both start and finish in the same spot so you go figure. Ride this trail twice – once in each direction!

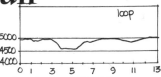

Options: First timers may want to play around on the Practice Loop (approx. 2.5 miles) before heading out on the Main Trail. It's a great way to introduce yourself to the terrain – similar only to that found on Mars – but not really any easier than the Main Loop. See separate description.

HINT: if you want to make the really steep bits, you need to ride with the nose of the saddle tickling your ... you know!

HINT #2: lower your tire pressure for better traction.

HINT #3: what do you want from me? the world?

Slickrock Bike Trail
— continued —

Directions: From Main x Center streets in town, head East on Center. Turn RIGHT on 400 East and follow to Mill Creek Drive. Turn LEFT on Mill Creek Drive. Turn LEFT at Sand Flats Rd. and follow it up the hill to the fee station. On the way you'll pass the Lion's Back Campground – you may get lucky and catch a view of a lunatic jeeper climbing Lion's back. They think we're crazy! The trail head parking lot is just around the curve on your left. Use the pit toilets and trash dumpster –check out the cool "wind dryers".

lunatic

Mountain Bike Museum of Moab

RIM CYCLERY

Rim Cyclery–The Hub of Cycling in Moab™
94 West 100 North St., Moab Utah 84532 (435) 259-5333
RIMCYCLERY.COM

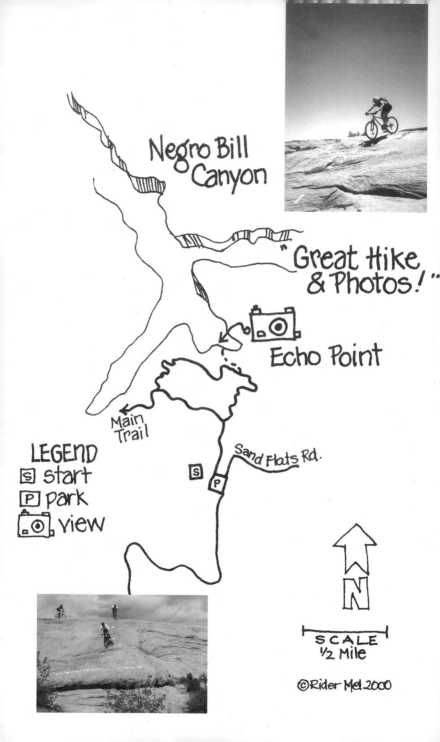

Negro Bill Canyon

"Great Hike & Photos!"

Echo Point

Main Trail

Sand Flats Rd.

LEGEND
S start
P park
view

N

SCALE
½ Mile

©Rider Mel 2000

Slickrock Practice Loop

short, tough
slickrock sampler

Distance:	2.5 Miles
Time Required:	½ to 1 Hour
Grunt Factor:	(6) Tough, but hey it's only 2½ miles
Techno Factor:	(9) Very Difficult. Steep Ups/Downs on ROCK
Fear Factor:	(8) Scary in spots
Route Finding:	Follow the painted white dashes. Dots go to overlooks!
Season:	Best spring/fall. Early morning ride in summer!

Description: The Practice Loop is kinda like a "quickie" - not as satisfying as 2 or 3 hours of sweating and grinding, but still a whole lot of fun. See the description of the Slickrock Main Trail. This loop starts in the same spot, but is much shorter (2.5 miles versus 13). If you've never ridden on slickrock before, do the practice loop first. It isn't really any easier than the Main trail, but it is a lot shorter and walking out isn't nearly as painful! Remember to keep the tire pressure a little lower than normal. On steep ups use the "power crunch" position –sphincter resting on nose of saddle. On downs place butt-crack over rear tire – not too close unless you like that kind of thing.

Options: This loop is a huge bag of fun to hike or take photos in the afternoon light. It's also a cool place to watch the sunset from – bring a flashlight!

Directions: From Main x Center streets in town, head East on Center. Turn RIGHT on 400 East and follow to Mill Creek Drive. Turn LEFT on Mill Creek Drive. Turn LEFT at Sand Flats Rd. and follow it up the hill to the fee station. The trail head parking lot is just around the curve on your left.

Spring Race Course

really hate yourself? try this one!

Distance: 26 Mile Loop
Time Required: 4 – 7 Hours
Grunt Factor: (10) Very Tough – mileage, climbing, grisly hike-a-bike
Techno Factor: (7) Amasa downhill is the toughest part
Fear Factor: (7) Some scary spots on downhill and hike-a-bike
Route Finding: Fairly Easy. Two key turns.
Season: Spring/Fall but NOT summer. This ride is long and hot in the best weather conditions. Bring all the water you can carry and some food.

Description: This is a long, grueling ride that is actually used as a race course each spring. You're basically taking Hurrah Pass, adding another 10 miles through Jackson Hole, carrying your bike up a big, nasty, 350 ft. portage straight up to the Amasa Back trail above, and downhilling back to Kane Creek Rd. and the trailhead. Sound like fun? The first 10 miles are a climb up to Hurrah Pass (exactly as described in the Hurrah Pass description). From there, you descend down the "back side" of the Pass and turn RIGHT towards Jackson Hole (and into a wash) at the 13 mile point. If you find yourself along the Colorado heading south, you've missed the turn. At the 18 mile mark you'll be damn close to the Jackson Hole monolith (big-ass butte-type rock thingy). Take the RIGHT turn. After another 2 miles, you should see a cairn marking the Jacob's Ladder portage. If you pass the power lines you have gone too far. Follow Jacob's Ladder up to the Amasa trail (I call this "racing technical" – you asked for it!) At the very top the hike-a-bike trail will run into the Amasa Back trail. Turn RIGHT to complete the loop and follow the mostly downhill back to Kane Creek Rd. At Kane Creek Rd. (after the rock staircase up) turn LEFT to reach the trail head.

Options: I suppose the truly demented could ADD some miles to this one by turning LEFT onto the Amasa Back Trail and

Spring Race Course Loop
continued

heading out to the overlook before descending. If that is appealing, you may want to do the whole loop twice (like the racers do)!

Directions: The trailhead for this "course" is identical to the one for the Hurrah Pass and Amasa Back rides. From Main x Center head SOUTH on HWY 191. Turn RIGHT at McDonalds onto Kane Creek Rd. Stay on Kane Creek past the Scenic Chairlift and around the curve. Go past the Moab Rim trailhead parking lot on your left. Park in the lot just before the cattle gate (where the pavement ends). Ride over the cattle gate and start timing your lap.

Counting the teeth after a crash

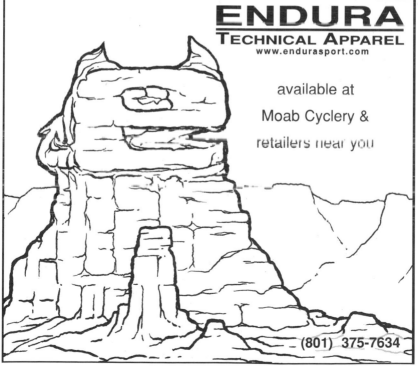

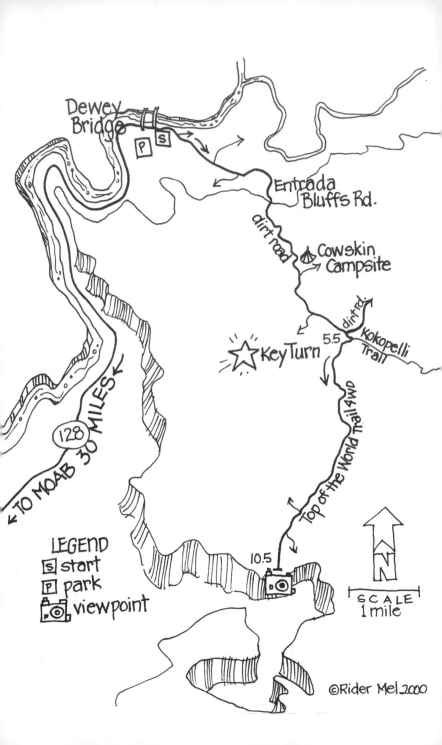

Dewey
Bridge

P S

Entrada
Bluffs Rd.

dirt road

Cowskin
Campsite

dirt rd.

5.5

Kokopelli
Trail

★ Key Turn

Top of the World Trail 4WD

128

←TO MOAB 30 MILES

10.5

LEGEND
S start
P park
📷 viewpoint

N

SCALE
1 mile

©Rider Mel 2000

Top of the World

crazy climb/descent with knee-buckling viewpoint

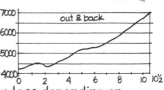

out & back

Distance:	21 Mile Out-and-back (or less depending on starting point)	
Time Required:	3 - 6 Hours	
Grunt Factor:	(10) A colossal 10-mile climb gaining 3,000+ ft. of elevation!	
Techno Factor:	(7) Relentless climb with lifts, rocks, corpses	
Fear Factor:	(7) Overlook and downhill return are the scariest parts	
Route Finding:	Easy. One slightly confusing turn.	
Season:	Spring/Fall. In the summer you need to start earlier than early. Bring as much water as you can carry.	

Description: This trail was designed for people who think body piercing is fun. From the trailhead the mostly boring climb gets more and more difficult until you feel like falling off the end of the earth. Just as you reach the point of wanting to throw yourself off a cliff – voila! (you reach the overlook, knucklehead!). As you climb, just keep repeating "this is gonna be one helluva downhill". The view from the top may even take the pain away. At over 2,500 ft. it is almost surreal – it looks more like a huge painting than reality! After numerous photos and snacks (you'll need them), turn around and retrace your steps at about 10x the speed. I once saw a guy get 8 flats on the downhill – you may want to add a little air pressure.

Directions: From town, drive North on Hwy 191. Turn RIGHT on Hwy 128. The drive along this Scenic Byway is pretty spectacular. After about 31 miles you will reach the Dewey Bridge Boat Launch. This is an ideal place to park if you intend to ride the full 21 miles. Otherwise, keep driving towards the Dewey bridge, turning RIGHT on the Kokopelli Trail/Entrada Bluffs Rd. just before you actually cross the bridge. Follow this gravel road for about 5½ miles to the start of the Top of the World trail and park. As you approach the trailhead intersection it can be confusing. The trail furthest to the right is the one you want.

MOAB
PHOTO LAB

- film
- cameras, binoculars
- tripods
- filters, batteries
- camera bags
- frames, albums

- Best Quality prints in just 3 hours
- Professional, friendly service
- Competitive Prices
- Monthly specials
- Open late 7 days a week in season

26 W. Center Moab, UT 84532
435-259-4181

Handy Dandy
Moab
Yellow Pages

area code
(435)

Bakeries
Knave of Hearts
84W 200N 259-4116
Red Rock Bakery
74 S Main 259-5941

Bed & Breakfast Accommodations
Blue Herron
900W Kane Creek................................259-4921
Desert Chalet
1275 San Juan Dr. 259-5793
Dream Keeper Retreat
191S 200E 259-5998
Mayor's House
505 Rosetree Ln 259-3019
Peach Tree Inn
1810 Shuman 259-4387
Sunflower Inn
185N 300E................................259-2974
Tomahawk
1162S Hwy 191................................259-8125

Bicycle Shops
Chile Pepper Bike Shop
702S Main 259-4688
Moab Cyclery
391S Main 259-7423
Poison Spider Bicycles
497N Main................................259-7882

Rim Cyclery   (see ad page 75)
94W 1stN 259-5333
                www.rimcyclery.com

Top of the World Cyclery (see ad page 67)
415N Main 259-1134
                www.twcmoab.com

Book Stores
Back of Beyond Books
83N Main 259-5154
TI Maps
29E Center 259-5529

Campgrounds
Canyonlands Campground
555S Main 259-6848
KOA Kampground
3225S Hwy 191...............................259-6682
Kane Springs Campground
1705S Kane Creek 259-8844
Moab Rim Campground
1900S Hwy 191...............................259-5002
Moab Valley Campark
1773N Hwy 191...............................259-4469
Portal RV Park
1261N Hwy 191 259-6108
Riverside Oasis
1861N Hwy 191...............................259-3424
Slickrock Campground   (see ad page 74)
130½N Hwy 191 259-7660
           www.slickrockcampground.com
Spanish Trail Campground
2980S Hwy 191...............................259-2411
Up The Creek Campground
210E 300S...............................259-6995

Camping/Outdoors Equipment
GearHeads
59S Main 259-3633
GearHeads
471S Main 259-4327
Moab Outdoors
Miller's Shopping Center...............................259-5731

Coffee Shops

Eklectica
352N Main...............................259-6896
Mondo Café
in McStiff's Plaza.....................259-5551
Peace Tree Café
20S Main 259-8503
Top of the World Cyclery
415N Main **259-1134**

Condo Rentals

Cottonwood/Fandango Condos
338E 100S.............................259-8897
Moab/Canyonlands (see ad below)
Reservations 800-505-5343
www.moabutahlodging.com
Red Valle Homes
201E 100N 259-5408

Westwood Guesthouse   (see ad page 55)
81E 100S 259-7283
www.moab-utah.com/westwood/guesthouse

Go Karts
Ya Gotta Wanna Go Karts
60W Cedar 259-8007

Groceries
City Market
425S Main................................259-5181

Hospital
Allen Memorial Hospital
719W 400N 259-7191
Emergency **911**

Hostels
Lazy Lizard Hostel
1213S Hwy 191 259-6057

Laundry Facilities
Moab Laundromat
702S Main 259-7456
Country Clean
588S Kane Creek 259-3987

Motels & Hotels
Aarchway Inn
1551N Hwy 191 259-2599
Apache Motel
166S 400E................................259-5727
Best Western Greenwell Inn
105S Main 259-6151
Big Horn Lodge   (see ad page 21)
550S Main......................**259-6171**
      www.bighornlodgemoabutah.com
Bowen Motel
169N Main 259-7132
Colorado River Lodge
512N Main 259-6122
Comfort Suites
800S Main 259-5252

Cottage Inn
488N Main 259-5738
Days Inn
426N Main 259-4468
Gonzo Inn
100W 200S 800-791-4044
Hotel Off Center
96E Center 259-4244
Inca Inn
570N Main 259-7261
J R's Inn
1075S Hwy 191 259-8352
Kokopelli Lodge
72S 100E 259-7615
Landmark Motel
168N Main 259-6147
Moab Ramada Inn
182S Main 259-7141
Moab Valley Inn
711S Main 259-4419

Prospector Lodge
186N 100W 259-5145
Red Stone Inn   **(see ad page 21)**
535S Main........................259-3500
www.moabredstone.com

Rustic Inn
120E 100S 259-6177
Silver Sage Inn
840S Main 259-4420
Sleep Inn
1051S Main 800-753-3746
Super 8 Motel
889N Main............................259-8868
Virginian Motel
70E 200S 259-5951

Pharmacies
City Market Pharmacy
425S Main 259-8971
Family Drug
90N Main 259-7771
Walker Drug
290S Main 259-5959

Photo Finishing
City Market
425S Main............................259-5181
Moab Photo Lab   **(see ad page 84)**
26W Center 259-4181

Restaurants
Arches Pancake Haus
196S Main 259-7141
Banditos Grill   **(see ad page 27)**
467N Main 259-3894
Bar-M Chuckwagon
7000N Hwy 191 259-2276
Branding Iron
2971S Hwy 191 259-6275
Breakfast at Tiffany's
90E Center 259-2553
Buck's Grill House
1393N Hwy 191 259-5201
Center Café

92E Center 259-4295
Eddie McStiff's
57S Main 259-2337
Expressa Pizza
1500N Hwy 191.........................259-2253
Fat City Smoke House
36S 100W 259-4302
Hogi Yogi
396S Main.................................259-2656
JB's of Moab
811S Main.................................259-2646
La Hacienda
574N Main 259-6319
Moab Brewery
686S Main 259-6333
Moab Diner
189S Main 259-4006
Pasta Jay's
4S Main 259-2900
Pizza Hut
265S Main 259-6345
Poplar Place
11E 100N.................................259-6018
Slickrock Café
5N Main 259 8004
Smitty's Golden Steak
540S Main 259-4848
Sunset Grill
900N Hwy 191 259-7146
Szechuan Restaurant
105S Main 259-8984

Search & Rescue 911

Shower Facilities
Canyonlands Campark
555S Main 259-6846
Lazy Lizard Hostel
1213S Hwy 191 259-6057
Moab Swim Center
181W 400N 259-8226
Moab KOA
3225S Hwy 191.................................259-6682
Moab Valley Campark
1773N Hwy 191.................................259-4469

Poison Spider Bike Shop
497N Main 259-7882
Slickrock Campground
130½N Hwy 191 ....**259-7660**
Up The Creek Campround
210E 300S 259-6995

Shuttle Services
Acme Bike Shuttle **260-2534**

Coyote Shuttle 259-8656

Roadrunner Shuttle **(see ad page 66)**
www.moab.net/roadrunner **259-9402**

Taverns/Clubs
Outlaw Saloon
44W 200N 259-2654
Rio Restaurant
2S 100W 259-6666

Theatres
Slickrock Cinemas
580 Kane Creek Blvd 259-4441

For corrections, errors or omissions, email
ridermel@moabtrailguide.com

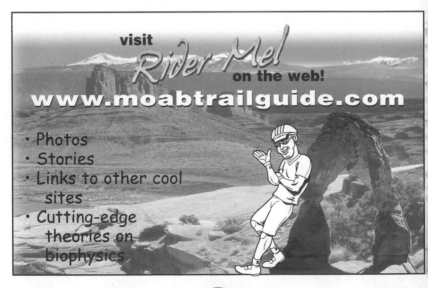

Things that ROCK

Chicks that ride
Trails that can hurt you
Mountain biking vacations
Silly facial hair (except on girls)
Downhills
Uphills
Big, nasty rocks
BIG burritos
24 hour City Market
Café Americanos
Beer
Manhattans

Things that SUCK

Muddy trails
People who ride muddy trails
Singletrack cops – bust you for
ridin if it ain't singletrack
Crashes
Weeks in recovery from crashes
Sand
Walking your bike
Trail craps
Running out of water
Rain
Fat kids who only ride downhill
Car rental agencies
Looking at new bikes when you can't afford one
ANYONE who reproduces this book
without permission.
© 2000 Rider Mel

Wall of Pain

More Crap
I'm not done spouting yet.

This endeavor has been exciting, fun, boring, depressing, frustrating and mostly scary as hell. You may not care, but this is my book – if you don't like this section, don't include one in YOUR book.

I rode the trails, made the maps, rode the trails, wrote the descriptions, rode the trails, and had hallucinations (some might call it "vision"). Heather rode the trails, schmoozed, rode the trails, and sold ads – she rode the trails too! Kristian made the cover look like Moab. Aiden made me look like a cartoon character. Brad made it look like a book. Joan put it all together and told me I "had horseshoes up my ass."

Thanks to Dave and Sheryl at TWC for friendship, comments and Americanos. More thanks to Dave and to Darryl The Destroyer for trail advice. Thanks to Thursday Louie for the adventure in the La Sals. Thanks to Ray for being Cosmic. Thanks to Heather, Phoenix and Cleo for missing me nearly as much as I missed you. Thanks to Mom for airmiles and emotional support. Thanks to the entire "Moab Crew" for being so dedicated and bizarre over the years. Thanks to the Auberge Lafferty gang for riding, comments and poetry reviews.

Hey guys,
it's about the riding!

the end